My Magic Dreadlocks

Enrico Miguel Thomas

My Magic Dreadlocks   .

ISBN   978-1-64552-194-5   (Paperback)
ISBN   978-1-64552-193-8   (Digital)

Lettra Press books may be ordered through booksellers or by contacting:

Lettra Press LLC
30 N Gould St. Suite 4753
Sheridan, WY 82801
1 307-200-3414 | info@lettrapress.com
www.lettrapress.com

My name is Malik and

I have dreadlocks. My hair is different!
It sticks up high and it is very long!

It sticks up so high that it can reach the stars
and planets!

My dreadlocks are magic!

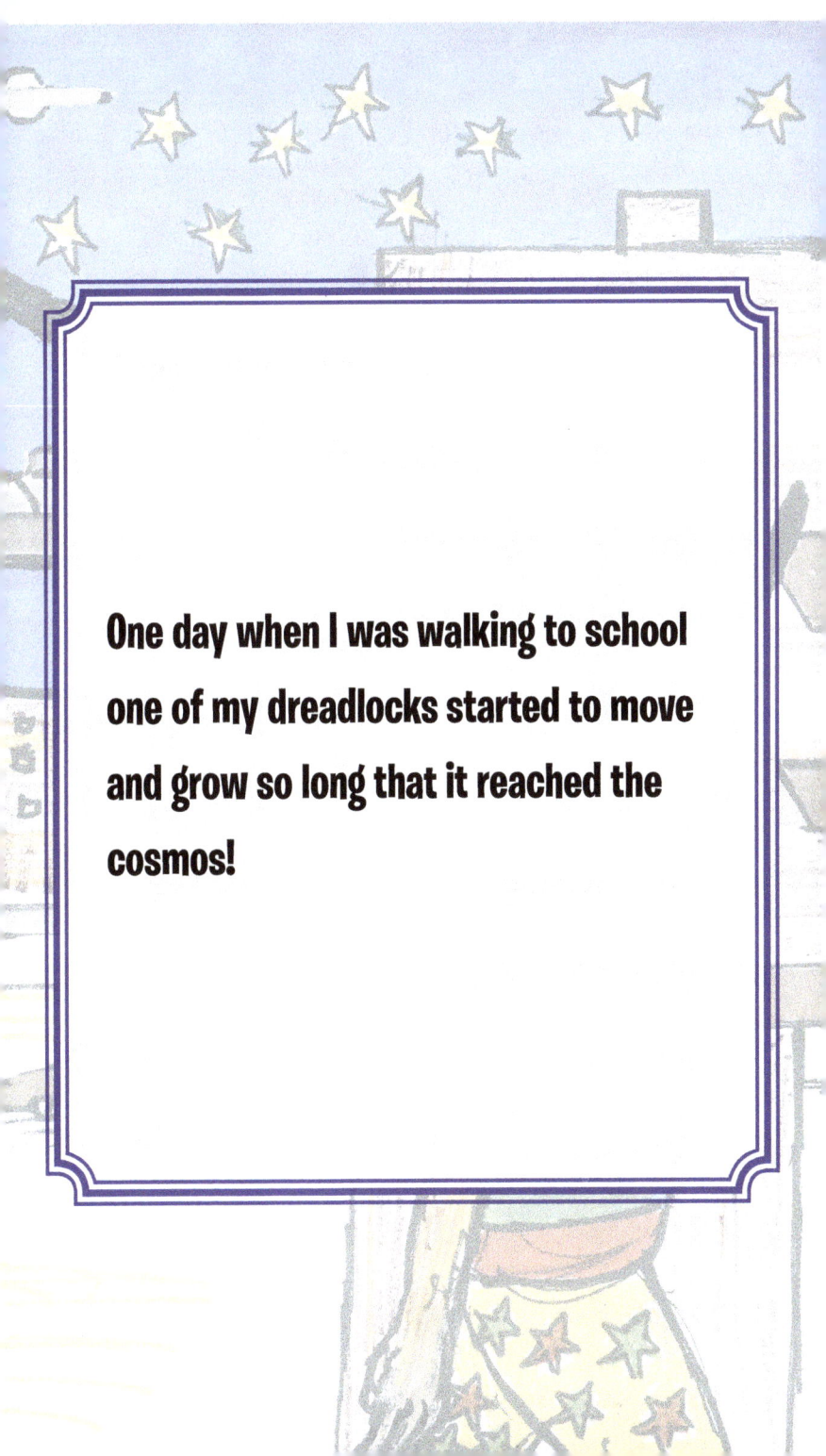

One day when I was walking to school one of my dreadlocks started to move and grow so long that it reached the cosmos!

Then in a flash I was transported to the stars!

I was so glad because on earth people make fun of me and call me names!

My dreadlocks began to communicate with the planets and stars all around me.

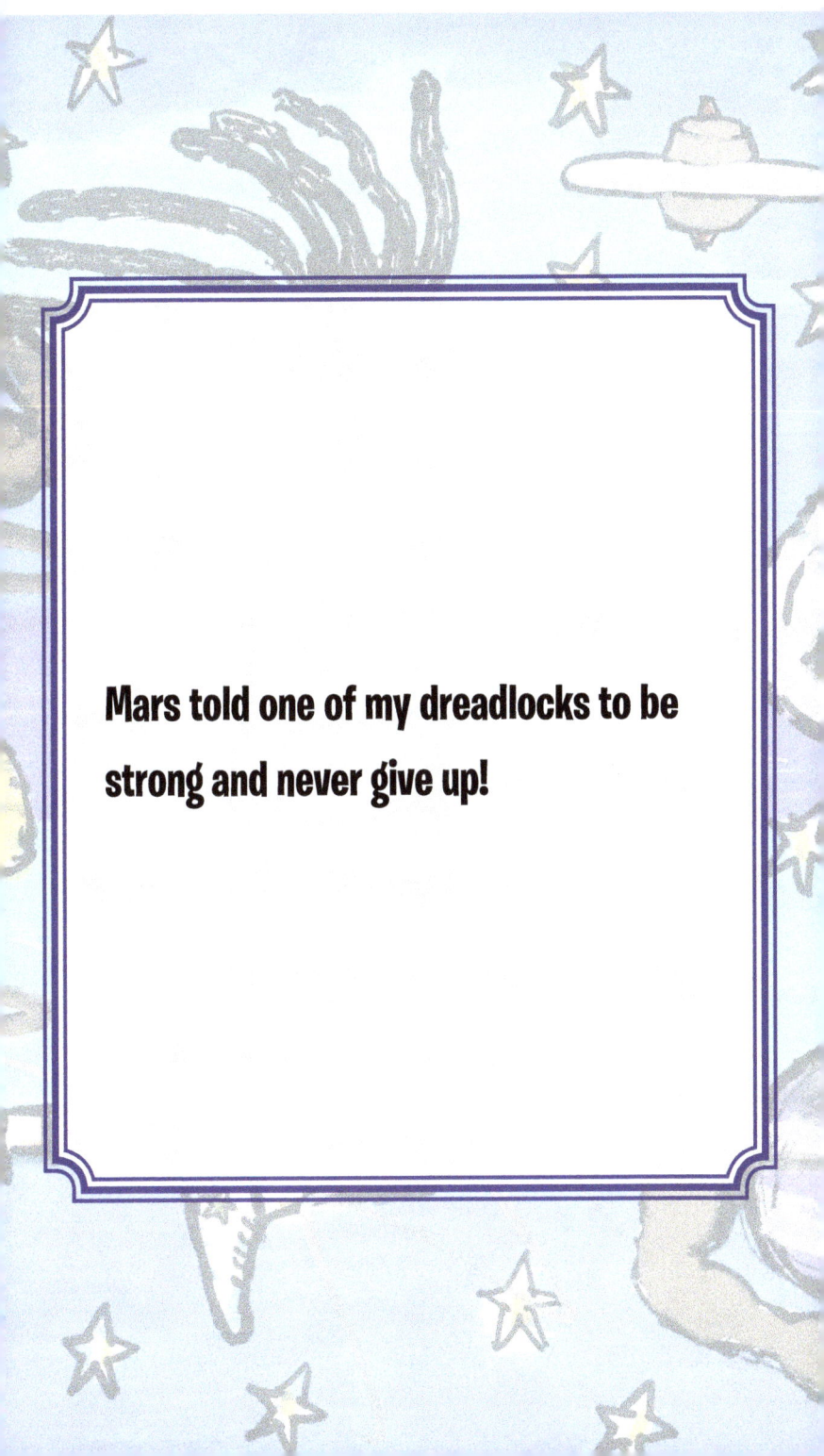

Mars told one of my dreadlocks to be strong and never give up!

Jupiter told another dreadlock to read more books and travel the earth.

Venus told another dreadlock to appreciate the beauty all around me.

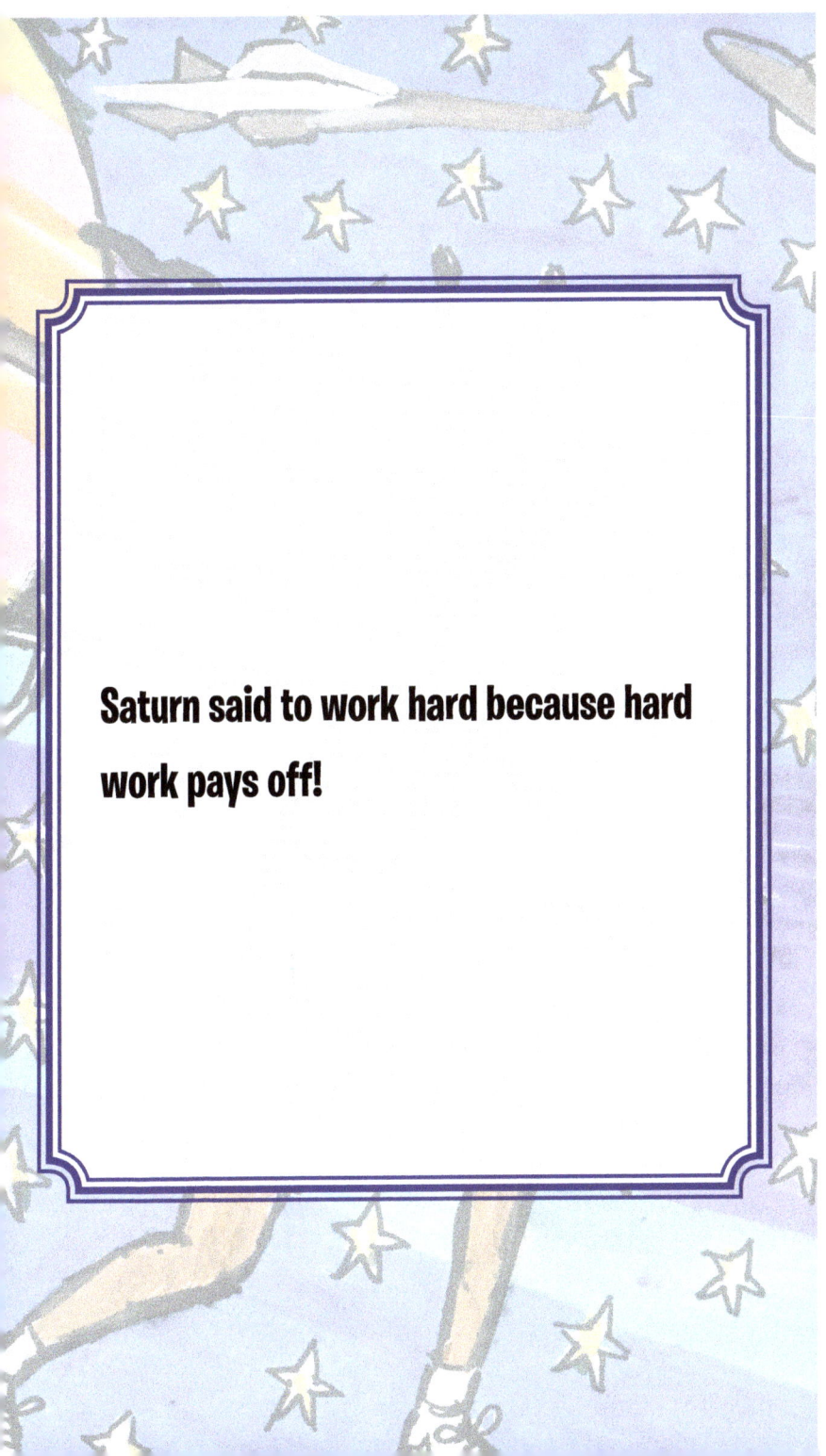

Saturn said to work hard because hard work pays off!

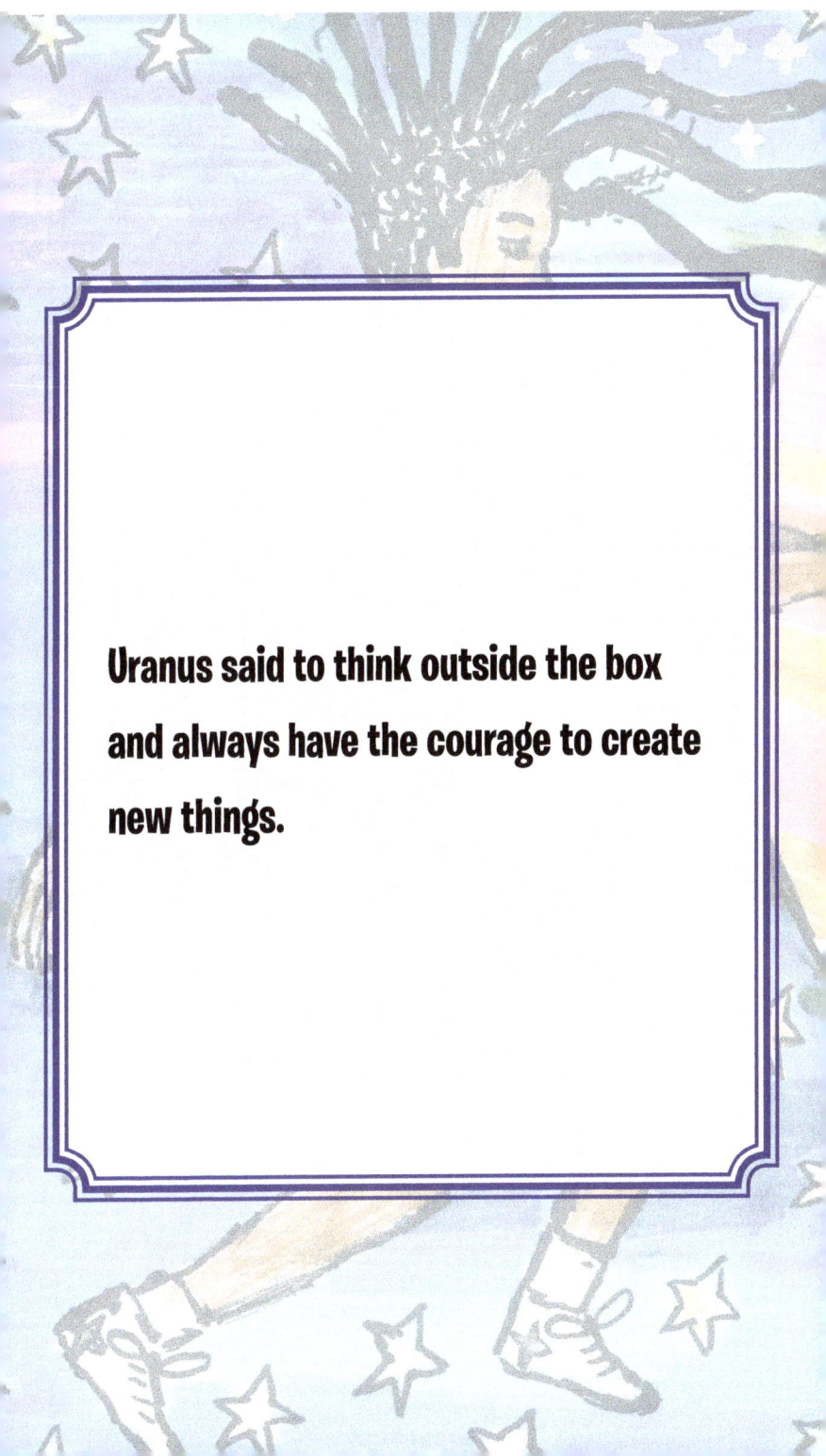

Uranus said to think outside the box and always have the courage to create new things.

Pluto said to ignore the box and go within!

Mercury was just to busy to talk.

Neptune said that all my dreams can come true!

Earth had the last message for my dreadlocks but the message was delayed?

Instead Earth decided to make me a big spaceship so that I can get back home.

Before I took off in the spaceship, Earth said that I should not let what people say bother me and that I still have work to do over there.

In a flash I was back on Earth again!

I said thank you to all my dreadlocks for the incredible journey, and told them that I was so happy to have my magic dreadlocks!

The End

Printed in the USA
CPSIA information can be obtained
at www.ICGtesting.com
LVHW062146301123
765241LV00103B/3975